MOTHER SAID

The author with his mother.

MOTHER SAID

poems by

HAL SIROWITZ

Crown Publishers, Inc.
New York

To the memory of my mother, Estelle.
And to my father, Milton.

Copyright © 1996 by Hal Sirowitz

Published by Crown Publishers, Inc., 201 East 50th Street, New York,
New York 10022. Member of the Crown Publishing Group.

Random House, Inc. New York, Toronto, London, Sydney, Auckland

CROWN is a trademark of Crown Publishers, Inc.

Manufactured in the United States of America

Design by Lauren Dong

Library of Congress Cataloging-in-Publication Data
Sirowitz, Hal.
Mother said : poems / by Hal Sirowitz. — 1st ed.
I. Title
PS3569.I725M68   1996   96-2440
811'.54—dc20   CIP

ISBN 0-517-70497-8

10   9   8   7   6   5   4   3

First Edition

ACKNOWLEDGMENTS

The author wishes to thank the National Endowment for the Arts and the MacDowell Colony for their support.

Some of the poems in *Mother Said* appeared previously in the following chapbooks: *Bedroom Wall* (Iniquity Press), *No More Birthdays* (Bacchae Press), *Fishnet Stockings* (Appearances), *The Morning After* (Butthead Press), *Two Second Kiss* (Mulberry Press), and *Happy Baby* (Bacchae Press).

Some of the poems in *Mother Said* appeared previously in the following magazines and anthologies: *Aloud: Voices from the Nuyorican Poets' Café, B City, The Big Spoon* (Northern Ireland), *Convulvulus, Corde, Digitas, Dog* (England), *Downtown, Earthwise Poetry Journal, Estero, Excursus, Exquisite Corpse, Footwork: The Paterson Literary Journal, A Gathering of the Tribes, Global Tapestry Journal* (England), *Hanging Loose, Home Planet News, Ikon, In Your Face, Java Journal, Lips, The Little Magazine, Long Shot, Membrane, Mosaic, Mudfish, Neruda Press* (Scotland), *New Letters, New Observations, New York Poets, Orphic Lute, Painted Bride Quarterly, The Quarterly, Rain Dog Review, Rant, Red Tape, Revival: Spoken Word from Lollapalooza 94, Sensitive Skin, Slipstream, Synaesthetic, Three Mile Harbor, True Wheel, Vox, We Speak for Peace, West Coast Magazine* (Scotland), *The Word Thursdays, Wu Wei, Yarrow, Yonkly* (Scotland), *Zenos* (England), and *Zone 3.*

CONTENTS

People ask me how you can tell a doll is dead and the answer is very simple. A doll is dead when you just can't play with it anymore.

SHIRLEY McCOY

WEEKLY WORLD NEWS, FEBRUARY 5, 1985

DAMAGED BODY

Don't swim in the ocean while it's raining,
Mother said. Lightning can hit the water,
& you'll be paralyzed. You don't like
to eat vegetables. Imagine having
to spend the rest of your life being one.
Someone will have to wash you,
take you to the bathroom, & feed you.
Children will tease you. But
you may be lucky, & get struck
by only a small voltage. Then you'll be
a smart vegetable, like an asparagus.
You'll be able to make your bed by yourself—
which you don't do now—but people
will feel too sorry for you to talk to you.
You may think it'll be fun to vegetate
around the house all day. But
every time you'll think about yourself,
like wouldn't it be nice to eat a chocolate
        ice cream cone,
the thought will flicker, & then go out.

CHOPPED-OFF ARM

Don't stick your arm out of the window,
Mother said. Another car can sneak up
behind us, & chop it off. Then your father
will have to stop, stick the severed piece
in the trunk, & drive you to the hospital.
It's not like the parts of your telescope
that snap back on. A doctor will have to sew it.
You won't be able to wear short sleeves.
You won't want anyone to see the stitches.

CRUMBS

Don't eat any food in your room,
Mother said. You'll get more bugs.
They depend on people like you.
Otherwise, they would starve.
But who do you want to make happy,
your mother or a bunch of ants?
What have they done for you?
Nothing. They have no feelings.
They'll eat your candy. Yet
you treat them better than you treat me.
You keep feeding them.
But you never offer me anything.

SONS

We're Jewish, Father said.
So we don't believe in Christ.
If God wanted us to worship Jesus
He would have arranged for us to be born
into an Italian family. I have nothing
against Him. He was probably a very nice man.
You have to give Him credit for trying.
A lot of people still believe He's the Son of God.
I don't know what He had against His real father.
But if you ever did that to me,
said you were someone else's son, I'd be insulted.

HOW I CAME TO BE

Father brushed his hair back
before he went to meet my mother
in the lobby of the Hotel Astor. He
waited under the clock. She
checked the buttons on her blouse
to make sure none were opened. Then
she walked toward him. They kissed.
They went to a dance. When the waiter
wasn't looking, my father kept pouring some Scotch,
that he hid in his pocket, into his soda.
He got drunk. She walked him to a park bench,
& fed him coffee & peanuts until he gradually
got sober. I wasn't born yet.
I was only a vague idea in their minds
that became clearer the more he walked her home.

REMEMBER ME

Every weekend your mother & I tour cemetery plots,
Father said, the way most people visit model homes.
We have different tastes. I like jutting hills
overlooking traffic, whereas she prefers a bed
of flowers. She desires a plot away from traffic noise.
I let her have her way in death to avoid a life of Hell.
But when you light memorial candles for us,
        arrange hers
in the center of a flowery tablecloth, but place mine
on the windowsill. Don't say any prayers for me,
just wet your finger, & pass it through the flame.
Remember me by the tricks I have taught you.

NO MORE BIRTHDAYS

Don't swing the umbrella in the store,
Mother said. There are all these glass jars
of spaghetti sauce above your head
that can fall on you, & you can die.
Then you won't be able to go to tonight's party,
or go to the bowling alley tomorrow.
And instead of celebrating your birthday
with soda & cake, we'll have
anniversaries of your death with tea
& crackers. And your father & I won't
be able to eat spaghetti anymore, because
the marinara sauce will remind us of you.

DEFORMED FINGER

Don't stick your finger in the ketchup bottle,
Mother said. It might get stuck, &
then you'll have to wait for your father
to get home to pull it out. He
won't be happy to find a dirty fingernail
squirming in the ketchup that he's going to use
on his hamburger. He'll yank it out so hard
that for the rest of your life you won't
be able to wear a ring on that finger.
And if you ever get a girlfriend, &
you hold hands, she's bound to ask you
why one of your fingers is deformed,
& you'll be obligated to tell her how
you didn't listen to your mother, &
insisted on playing with a ketchup bottle,
& she'll get to thinking, he probably won't
listen to me either, & she'll push your hand away.

MISSING FINGER

Don't stick your hand in the water,
Mother said, while your father is rowing.
A fish might think that one of your fingers is a worm—
I heard that the constant water in their eyes
makes them nearsighted—& bite it off.
Then you won't be able to count to ten
on your fingers, & you'll flunk
all your math tests. And you won't
be able to get a good grip on your baseball bat,
& what would have been a home run
will now become a single. And don't think
that just because you'll have one less fingernail
to cut, we'll make your life easier, & treat you
like a cripple. Your remaining fingers
must learn to work harder.

A DOG'S BRAIN

Just because my dog jumps up to kiss you,
she said, each time you enter the house,
doesn't mean that she knows what she's doing.
She probably learned that behavior from me, saw me
kissing you, & thinks that's the right thing
to do, but she saw me doing it before I knew
you were a jerk, & she can't make that distinction.

A DOG'S HEART

The only reason I've stayed with you
this long, she said, was because if I
broke up with you, it would have hurt
my dog, who has grown to depend on you
for her daily walks & meals, whereas
since you never did anything for me—
luckily I'm able to walk & feed myself—
it's hard for me to miss you, but
I'm sure I will, because each time I hear
my dog bark, she might be asking for you.

MY THOUGHTFUL SON

I can't kill myself, Mother said,
because it's prohibited by Jewish law,
so I'm relying on you to do it for me,
& you've been doing a good job. You
already took a few days off my life
when you got mud on your shoes,
& left a trail all over the house. I had
to get on my knees to scrub the floor,
& I thought to myself, My son is
only trying to be kind, he's shortening
my life so I won't have to worry
about old age, but if he really cared
about me, he'd put an end to me right now.

NOT TALKING TO ME AGAIN

Beauty is only skin deep, Father said,
but don't tell your mother I told
you that or she'll think I'm saying
that she's ugly. But I didn't marry her
just for her looks. I married her
because I thought that she was kind.
I happen to be wrong tonight. But
that doesn't mean I won't be right tomorrow.

MY DEAD GOLDFISH

I wanted an alligator for a pet,
but my parents got me a goldfish.
When he died my mother flushed him down the toilet.
She said if we bury him in the yard
a cat might dig him up & eat him.
I was mad at my father for using the bathroom
ten minutes after the burial.
He had no respect for the dead.

TWO VISITS IN ONE DAY

We're going to the cemetery to visit
some dead relatives, Mother said, & on the way
back we'll stop over at your aunt's house.
It's good practice to mix the living
with the dead. Otherwise, we'd end up
either being bored at the cemetery, or if
we stayed too long at her house, we'd wish
that she was dead. This way by doing
two things in one day we can do something fun
the next weekend, like go to the beach.
If your aunt keeps talking too much, like she
usually does, we'll tell her that we just got
back from the cemetery, & that should shut her up.
She never goes there, & it shows, because
the more you visit the dead the less you have to say.

HORNS ON YOUR HEAD

The further you venture from the house,
Mother said, the fewer people you'll know.
Everyone on this block has either heard
of you or has seen you at one time. But
on the next block maybe only one person
will recognize you. Then there are hundreds
of blocks where no one knows you exist.
And it goes on that way until you get
to Nebraska, where it gets even worse.
There, the people never met a Jew before.
They think you have horns, & will want
to look for them. That's why you should never move
too far away from me. You don't want
strangers to always be touching your head.

BREAKING UP IS HARD TO DO

"We don't have anything in common,"
I said. "We're two completely different people.
It doesn't make sense to stay together."
But then she started to rub my penis
through my pants, & I suddenly remembered
that we both did like Indian food.

SERENADE

We sat so close together on the subway
a policeman walked up to us,
took out his nightstick,
put it under his chin like a violin,
& pretended he was serenading us.
That was the year we loved each other
so much he could have arrested us for it.

EMERGENCY SITUATION

I threw out your blue underwear,
Mother said. It had a hole in it.
No son of mine will ever be caught wearing that.
It's a reflection on me. It makes me look bad.
I know no one can see it. But you can't be sure.
Let's say you break your leg. You're rushed
to the hospital. The nurse takes off
your pants. She'll see it. The doctor
may not even put on a cast, because
he'll think you come from a poor family.
I didn't bring you up to embarrass me.
When you were little I dressed you up
as a girl. You were gorgeous.
You had curls hanging over your face.
But let's be honest. You're no longer cute.
You're too old to get away with anything.

BODY PARTS

Keep your hand inside the railing,
Mother said, when you ride the escalator.
I read once in some out-of-town newspaper
about this boy who got his index finger
chopped off doing what you are doing.
His parents rushed him to the hospital,
but in all their excitement they forgot
to bring the chopped-off finger with them.
They went back to get it, but it was gone.
Probably some cleaning woman threw it away.
The doctors had to sew someone else's finger
to the stump, & I heard that it doesn't match,
that he wears gloves even in the summer.

DOES GOD EXIST?

There's no proof that God is up there,
Mother said. But no one can prove
that He isn't. Only the dead know.
But they're too busy being dead
to tell us. So if I were you
I would go to temple, & play it safe.
If He's dead all you lose is the time
you spent praying. But if He exists
& you didn't go, you'll be in big trouble.
You won't like it in Hell.
You never liked hot weather.
And then how can I visit you?
Angels aren't allowed inside.

THE START OF THE DAY

I didn't have to go to school to learn how
to become a mother, Mother said. It just came
naturally. If I put a bottle
in your mouth, you were happy. If I
pulled it out too quickly, you cried.
And if I left you alone, you were bored.
That's why I'm surprised that after all
these years, you still don't know how to act
like a son. While I was learning all these things
about you, you were learning nothing about me.
The one thing you should have learned is that I
hate to walk into your room, & see
your bed unmade. To me, that's like
never beginning the day. The morning
only starts after you've made your bed.

NIGHT TRICKS

I never think when I'm in bed,
Father said. I put myself under the sheets
to forget about the day. When
I was younger I used to toss & turn
thinking of ideas that could help me in business.
Once I stayed up all night, & in the morning
I rushed to my boss to tell him my plan
on how to make us rich. He laughed at me.
I felt like a jerk. The night plays tricks
on you. It makes you think you're smarter
than you are. That's why I always go
to bed early, & let your mother stay up late.

SPEAKING FOR HER DOG

You bought my dog a new collar,
she said, which she thanks you for,
& which I also thank you for. She wants
what all dogs want, love & to be fed
on time, which you do for her, but
she'll be a lot happier if you also
gave her owner, me, something nice
to wear, instead of just giving me kisses,
which I can get anytime I want
from her, & she has a bigger tongue.

TEACHING MY DOG

When I was in love with you, she said,
& my dog would lick & kiss your hand,
I thought she had good taste, but
when I got angry at you, & she
still followed you wherever you went,
I thought she had bad taste, & was
embarrassed that she might have learned it
from me. And if I yelled at you,
& kicked your shoes around the house,
I want you to know that I was doing it
for her, so she'd know what to do, & not
be submissive, if she fell in love
with another dog who was a jerk.

TELEVISION EXPERIENCE

I don't have your education,
Father said, but that doesn't mean
I'm not smart. It means that I've
learned everything by myself.
This is a wonderful country.
I don't like you knocking it.
The closest you've been to Vietnam
is the television set. You're no
expert on it. If you're so smart
you'd have found a way of going
to school without costing me any money.

HOW TO PRAY

Don't pray for material things,
Mother said, like a new football helmet.
God doesn't like that. Save Him
for bigger things, like if one of us
gets very sick. The way to get
on His good side is to ask for
general things, like health & happiness.
And tell Him he doesn't have to give them
to you now, you'll take them in the future.

WORD POWER

I could have tried to have another son,
Mother said, but then I'd have to divide
my love in two, so I sacrificed,
& just had you. But sometimes I think
you could have used the competition
that a baby brother would have brought.
All the relatives would put him in their arms,
& hold him high over their heads. And that just might
stir you to action. Because right now
you're even too lazy to look up a word
in the dictionary, & your vocabulary is limited.
And one day your wife is going to ask you
if you really love her. And you should
tell her yes, & that you also idolize her.
But since you don't know what that word means,
you won't be able to use it. And even if
she buys you *Webster's Unabridged Dictionary*
for a birthday present, you still might not get the hint.

KINDNESS

You need children who will take care of you
when you're old, Mother said, not that
I expect you to take care of me when
I get old. If you'd only learn how
to take care of yourself, & hold a steady job,
I'll be happy. I don't expect you
to support me when I'm old, though
I should hope you'd want to pay me back
in kindness for bringing you into this world.
You don't have to give me all the kindness now,
you can spread it out over the years.
If it wasn't for me you'd never have had
a life, but would have been stuck
inside your father's sperm cell with no way to get out.
I never charged you for raising you, but
maybe if I made you pay me every time
I taught you some manners, you might have
     learned some.

LOCKED DOOR

I was waiting for the house to catch on fire,
so I could wake up my parents &
save their lives. Then they'd have to
love me more. But the house didn't
burn, & I don't know what my parents
were doing behind the locked door
of their bedroom, but I just knew
that they weren't thinking about me. They kept
putting me to bed earlier, even when I wasn't
tired, because they said they needed more sleep,
but in the morning they never looked well rested.

NEWS OF MY DEATH

If you stay over at some girl's house,
Mother said, call me up, & give me
her phone number. If I happen to
drop dead, I want you to hear about it
from someone in your family, instead
of finding out about it by reading
some obituary in *The Daily News*.
You can bring her to the funeral too,
if she wants to go, but you should
go home first, & change your clothes.
Be sure to wear a black jacket & tie.
Take care of your father, & make sure
he doesn't drop dead too, worrying
if you're still alive. And if I
only happen to get a heart attack,
& want you to visit me in the hospital,
I promise not to embarrass you when I call
by telling her that I'm your mother.
I'll just say that I live next door to you.

DANGEROUS KISSING

I took you to a park that was so dangerous
that you had to hold on to your pocketbook
while kissing me. And I thought
that if you were risking your life to kiss me,
surely you'd take me back to your apartment
where it was safe. But you must have liked danger.

DIRECTLY NORTH OF ME

After we ate the stuffed eggplant
at the Turkish restaurant my penis
started acting like the needle
on a compass. It kept pointing
to you. But you kept looking
the other way. You weren't
interested in being found.

TRIAL AND TRIBULATION

Don't stick your finger in the electric socket,
Mother said. You could get a shock,
& if it doesn't kill you, it'll leave
a lot of static in your hair.
It might not come out with shampoo.
Your hair will stand straight on your head,
& everyone will know what you did.
If God didn't want you to have curly hair
He'd have given you to a different mother.
But He gave you to me, & I wonder why.
I went to temple. I said my prayers.

A BUM'S LIFE

You're going to be a bum, Mother said,
if you're not one already, but you'll
soon find out that even a bum
has to work hard convincing people
that he's really poor. When it rains
you can't stand out there holding
an umbrella, & ask for money, but
you have to get wet, because the more
you drip, the more sympathy you'll get,
& if you take a shower you won't
be able to use soap, because if there isn't
any dirt on your face, you won't look
authentic, & if someone gives you
a stale piece of bread, you'll have to
eat it, even if you're not hungry,
or you'll get a reputation for being
too choosy, & then no one will give you anything.
And the only favor I'll ask of you, if
you decide to make that your occupation,
is if I see you on the street,
& put a few dollars in your hand,
don't act like you know me, because
I don't want anyone to know that I'm your mother.

TWO BURIALS FOR THE SAME PERSON

According to Jewish law, Mother said,
if your arm gets chopped off,
you can't just throw it away, but
you have to bury it in a cemetery, because
it's considered a part of you. And
you can't have a tombstone for your arm
in New York, & then another one for your body
in New Jersey. All the parts of you
are supposed to be buried in the same place.
So, if you lost your arm when you lived
in New York, & then you happened to die
in California, your surviving relatives
couldn't bury you there, but would have to fly
you all the way back to New York,
so you'd be reunited with your arm.
And just because you're dead doesn't mean
the airline will let you fly for free.

WAR IN THE HOUSE

This used to be a quiet family,
Mother said, until you brought Vietnam
into the house. I don't want the war
in my living room. If you & your father
want to argue about it, then do it
in the backyard. There's plenty of room
back there. We hardly use it. It's about time
we got some use out of it. And if both of you
get tired of yelling & decide to do something useful
for a change, then you can always pick up
        the dead leaves.

ONE THING LEADS TO ANOTHER

While I was putting your underwear
in the wash, Mother said, I noticed
some brown stains, which can only mean
that you're not using enough toilet paper
when you go to the bathroom. And when
you leave the house & get a wife,
she won't be related to you, except
by marriage, so she won't be as tolerant
as I am. You don't want her to do separate washes,
one for her clothes, another for yours,
because that'll get her into the habit of doing
other things separately, like eating. And
once she realizes how much more enjoyable it is
not to eat with you, & not to have to hear you
chomp on your hamburger, she might try not to
live with you too, which means divorce.

MORE LIPSTICK

I wondered why she kept putting on more lipstick,
because when we kissed it was only
going to come off. But I guess
she knew what she was doing,
because when it came time to say
goodnight I only got a hug.

THE RELATIONSHIP EXPERT

I told my therapist that I had a girlfriend.
She told me not to worry about anything,
that I could count on her to help me,
because she was an expert on relationships,
& had been married for more than twenty years.
She said that the best approach is to always
downplay yourself, & boost the other person's ego.
She said that her husband & she are both doctors,
but she tells him that he's the better doctor,
& that if she ever got very sick she'd only
let herself be treated by him. So I told
my girlfriend that she was much better at sex
than I was. She said that she already knew that.

THE HOT STOVE

Mother was like a juggler,
she could cook five things
at the same time, & if she made
a mistake, one dish was overcooked,
she wouldn't be deterred,
she would just balance it out,
serve something a little raw.

GENIUS

That isn't a picture of a girl,
Mother said. That's Albert Einstein.
He's different from us. He's a genius.
He's allowed to wear his hair that long.
You're not supposed to make fun of him.
If you ever become that smart
you don't have to get a haircut either.
But believe me, it isn't worth it.
It's hard to manage. You have to comb
it twice as long to get all the knots out.

FINDING YOUR WAY BACK HOME

Don't lean on the display window,
Mother said. It might shatter,
& if by some lucky miracle
you don't get hurt, the manager
of the store will make me pay for it.
At first I'll try to pretend that I'm not
your mother, but the urge to smack you
will probably be greater than the act
of disownment. And how would you
get back home if I sneaked away?
I keep imploring you to look at
street signs once in a while,
it might even improve your reading score.

BROKEN GLASS

Make sure you don't break another glass,
Mother said, while you're drinking your milk.
When Moses broke the Ten Commandments,
not only did he have to climb the mountain again
to get new ones, but God punished him
by making him wait before he could visit
the Promised Land. And maybe I should let you
drink only out of paper cups, & make you wait
until you own your own home to use glass.
You should be thankful that I'm a lot nicer than God.

CEMETERY PLOT ECONOMICS

When I bought you a cemetery plot
for a birthday present, Father said,
instead of thanking me & acting grateful
you said you didn't want it,
that you weren't ready to die.
But you can't prepare for death.
It takes you when it wants to.
And the most you can do is make sure
that when it comes it doesn't cost you
an arm & a leg. If you wait until you're dying
to buy one you may not have the time.
You might not want to be bothered.
The salesman will know you're near death,
& he'll charge you a whole lot more.

GIRLFRIEND OVER FOR DINNER

She's very pretty, Mother said,
but she's going to leave you.
She was talking about the future,
& you weren't in it, so I asked her
to tell it to me again, just in case
she made a mistake & left you out,
but you weren't in the second version either.
She talked about going away to school,
& when I asked her what she was planning
to bring with her, she talked about her coat,
her boots, but she never mentioned you.
She says she's very fond of you, but people
say that about puppies they're about to give away.

WHAT DID HE DO DIFFERENT?

At the party his hands were on your breasts.
But when we went out together,
you only let me touch your coffee cup.

THE MORNING AFTER

When I opened the shades
I remember God saying,
Let there be light,
& there was light,
so I said to her, Let's
not break apart, & she said,
Give me time to think about it,
I can't make fast decisions.

REVENGE

Mother wouldn't let me sleep
with my head next to the open window.
She didn't want me to catch a cold.
So when I had trouble falling asleep
I could feel the wind tickling my feet.
There was nothing to do that summer,
but pretend I was dead.
I wished I could still see her after I died,
so I could watch her miss me.
But I kept saving up my death
until it had more value.
The more people I knew, the more would cry.

DIRTY DIAPERS

I could never understand how the Germans
could hate us, Mother said, just because
we were Jewish, but what's even harder
for me to understand is that you could
hate me just because I'm your mother.
Someone has to tell you to go to bed early,
& if I don't, & you fall asleep in class, your teacher
could tell a social worker from a child abuse agency,
& they could take you away from me,
which might not be that bad if it was
only for a weekend, because I could use
a rest from you, but if it was for
a longer period of time, it'd slowly kill me.
I hope you know that you were a planned child,
your father & I really wanted you, even though
we weren't sure what we were getting.
You weren't an accident, though before
you were toilet trained you had plenty
of those. And I had to clean it up,
though I never once held it against you,
it just took you a while to develop
the proper sphincter control, & I thought
that when you got older you could make it up
to me, & clean the bathroom for me once in a while.

THE DOUBLE

Father said he was watching the news,
& saw someone at the antinuclear demonstration
who looked a lot like me. He
had my nose, same color hair,
& was wearing my coat. But he knew
it couldn't have been me, because
this guy was waving at the television camera,
flashing the peace sign, embarrassing
his poor mother & father, & not showing
too much smarts. For why make it easy
for those FBI agents to identify you?
They get good pay, so let them
do a little work by covering your face,
& wearing someone else's coat.

GOD'S GOOD SIDE

You're a disgrace to the Jews,
Mother said, if you don't tuck in your shirt.
There are people out there who hate us,
because some of us are rich & smart.
And now you want them to hate us,
because we dress sloppy. We have
enough enemies. We don't need you
to make new ones. And I don't like
you talking to your friends during
the rabbi's sermon, because if we need to ask
a favor from God, He may not listen
to you or your father, who falls asleep
during the service, but He might just listen
to the rabbi, especially this year, since he
just built a new temple for Him.

FIRST & LAST TIME

I was nervous when we got into bed,
because the first time you do something
you set a pattern that is hard to break.
I thought we might make love the same way
for the rest of our lives. But I didn't
have to worry. We never slept together again.

EYES ARE EVERYWHERE

Now that you're getting older, Mother said,
you'll have to wear a jockstrap,
like your father, when you go to the beach.
You might look at a girl leaning over
in her bathing suit, & suddenly get a boner.
You can't always hide it by running into
the ocean, some people can see under water.

SCORECARD

I fell in love with her sitting down,
& I'm sure if I was standing,
I would have fallen in love with her standing,
but we were sitting, & by the time
I stood up I was no longer in love with her,
& she was never in love with me, sitting or standing.

MY FIFTH RELATIONSHIP

I didn't feel relaxed enough
to use her bathroom. I
waited until I left her apartment.
She gave me my own towel,
but I felt more at home in a public toilet.
No one cared if I left water on the floor.

 63

READING LESSON

To become a better reader, Mother said,
you have to read everything you see. If
you're walking in the street you should be
reading the traffic signs. If you're
in a restaurant you should read
the breakfast menu even if you're only there
for dinner. The world is one big book.
Words are everywhere. They're in your shoe
& on the label of your underwear.
And when you get to be older you'll
be able to read facial expressions.
But let me warn you now that if a girl
happens to smile at you that doesn't mean
you should be reading a lot into it.

LIVING AT HOME

It's impossible for your parents to take you
to court, my therapist said, & sue you
for the money they spent buying you shoes.
The law states that they had to provide for you.
So if they tell you they want you to reimburse them
for all the pants they had to buy you
don't tell them to sue you, because that'll be
confrontational. You should just humor them,
& say that when you get a job you'll send them
checks in the mail. Don't tell them how much
you're going to give them. The way to avoid
a crisis is to always speak in general terms.
You can get specific after you leave the house.

THE COLLECTOR

I know you tell your therapist,
Mother said, all these bad stories
about me, making me look like
a villain. But if she ever came
to the house, & took a look at your room,
she'd have bothered you too to clean it.
Other sons collect stamps & coins,
but I had to have one who collected dust.
It wouldn't have been so bad if you kept
your collection under your bed, but you
spread it around the house whenever
        you left your room.

THERAPIST NEAR THE HOUSE

You should see a therapist, Mother said,
who lives close to me instead of having
to go all the way into the city. After
you see him you can have lunch with me.
I'll tell you whether he gave you the right advice.
And if you don't want to tell me what he said
that's okay too. I'm used to it. Though it was
easier to take when you were three, & could
hardly talk. When you got older I thought
you'd be more profound. You tell a stranger
your life story. But when you visit me you shut up.

PARENT SWAPPING

We know you don't appreciate us,
Mother said, & that you'd rather have
different parents, like the Goldbergs
who live across the street. You think
we're cruel, because we make you go to bed early.
But if another family will take you
we'll be happy to get rid of you. Though
after a few days you'll want to come back.
No one is like your natural parents. And anyway
you're no bargain. You don't make your bed.
You get dirt all over the house. But I'm
too nice a person to tell the neighbors
what's wrong with you. I just tell you.

AT MY GRAVE

Today we're going to visit my mother's grave,
Mother said, to give you practice
visiting a cemetery, so when I die,
& you visit me, you'll know what to do.
Don't go to my grave, say hello
& goodbye, & then leave. You should
stay there for a while, walk around
the other stones, so when you come back
again, I'll be easier to find. In fact,
whether I like it or not, all the people
buried next to me are my neighbors,
so you should say a prayer for them too.
Only think about the good things
I've done for you, & if I did bad things,
it wasn't on purpose, so you should
start forgetting about them now, so when
I die, there'll be less for you to forget.

BIRDS OF THE SAME FEATHER
FLOCK TOGETHER

If I wanted an animal for a son,
Mother said, I'd have looked for
an animal for a husband, but I didn't,
so don't disappoint me by turning into
a wolf, & chasing after every woman
you meet. You should be going only
to temple dances, & meeting Jewish women.
Mixed marriages work only if you
don't have any children, but once
you have one, you'll start fighting
with your wife about what religion the child
should be raised in, & then her parents
will start mixing in, & will encourage her
to cook you ham, & whatever else you don't like,
for dinner every night, so you'll stay away.

CHOW MEIN

Lots of people make a big commotion
about sex, Mother said, but after you
do it, then it's over. It doesn't last
as long as the chicken chow mein
you can order in a restaurant, because
at least after you're finished eating
some of it, you can have the waiter
put the rest of it in a doggie bag,
& can have it later when you get home.
Sex doesn't get you anything, unless
you decide to have a family. Though you should
get married first, because the woman
can always say it's not your child,
that she had it from someone else, &
then you'll be where you started, with nothing.
And even if you were lucky enough to have
twins, that doesn't mean she'll let you keep one.

SOUVENIRS

I had two French condoms, but you said
you'd rather just hold me, that if we had sex,
I'd only get frustrated. You fell asleep before
I could convince you otherwise. If we
had made love, I'd have just thrown them away,
but now I have them to remember you by.

CHANGE OF HEART

I wasn't sure if you'd sleep with me
even when our clothes were off. I
thought you might change your mind,
like you did at the Chinese restaurant,
first ordering fried shrimp, & then minutes after
the waitress left, wanting to have scallops instead.

MAGNIFIED

My parents got me a magnifying glass
for a present. I went into my room,
pulled down my pants, & made my penis
twice as large. The further away I held
the magnifying glass, the larger my penis became,
until it was thicker than my arm.
I looked around my room to see if there was
anything I could do with a gigantic penis,
but had no ideas. I pulled up my pants,
& went to the kitchen where Mother said,
"Do you like your new toy?" I told her that I did,
but I wished that the thing I was magnifying
stayed large even after I took the magnifying
        glass away.
"I wouldn't care for that," she said.
"The house is already messy.
I wouldn't want it to be a bigger mess."

HOW TO BE ROBBED

If someone on the street pulls a knife
on you, Father said, & asks for all
your money, give it to him, because
you can always make more, but you can't
get a new life. Let him have your change too,
even the pennies. Tell him that you understand
that he's robbing you only because
he has to, & that you're not angry at him,
or he might decide to kill you, so
there won't be a witness. If he starts
playing with the blade, offer him
your wristwatch too. You can always
get another one. I'd give him
my ring, too, if he asks, but
don't volunteer to give him anything else,
like your coat & shoes, because he might become
attached to you, especially if they fit him,
& he could decide to follow you home,
& if he does, he'll rob me too.

SPYING INSTRUCTIONS

Go downstairs to the den, Mother said,
& tell me what your sister & her boyfriend
are doing. If they're necking, I want to know.
And if they're not kissing, I need to know
what they're arguing about. If you
get caught, don't tell her that I told you
to do it. Just tell her that you had to use
the bathroom downstairs, because I was
in the one upstairs, & that you stopped to listen,
because you're curious to know what it'll be
like when you get older. The worst that can
happen is that she'll punch you, & that'll
give me the excuse to go downstairs, yell
at her for hurting you, & find out for myself
why those two have been down there for so long.

ONCE IS ENOUGH

Don't go too near the cliff, Mother said,
because you could fall off, & then
it'll be the end of the world
as you know it, & the beginning
of it as only God knows it, & He
won't be too happy with you,
because I'm sure He put you here
for a purpose, or He wouldn't
have made it possible for me to have you,
& when He finds out that you ended your life
prematurely, He might want to send you back,
but you won't be coming back through me,
I'm too tired to have any more children.

LET ME DIE FIRST

It's not enough that I had to suffer
terrible labor pains, Mother said,
to bring you into this world, but
looking at your bloodshot eyes
I can tell you've been taking drugs,
& you'll probably die before I do,
& then I'll have to mourn you too.
I thought you would at least have
the decency to die after me, so
you can put flowers on my grave,
& light memorial candles for me.
But I see that I'll just have to
find someone else to do that for me.
And even if you do happen to survive me,
you probably destroyed so many brain cells
that you won't be able to find
the cemetery that I'm buried in,
because they're usually in out-of-the-way places,
since people don't want to be reminded of death.

DECLARATION

If John F. Kennedy can take his mother
to his inauguration, Mother said, & not feel
ashamed when she puts her arm around him,
then how come you don't want to be seen
with me on the street? He's the Commander-in-Chief
of the entire country, & you're not even in charge
of your room. I have to clean it for you.
I never heard anyone call him a sissy
for hanging around his mother, & even if
someone did, it wouldn't bother him, because
he knows it's not true. You never told me
to get lost when I was putting on your diapers.
Mothers are the most maligned group in the country.
As soon as their children get big enough,
they pretend that they don't know us anymore.

ALL IN THE FAMILY

Don't lean against the car door,
Mother said. It may not be locked,
& you can fall out. You're no use
to us dead, & even though you're not
much use to us now, hopefully when
you get older we'll be able to find
some use for you. If you become
a doctor you can check my blood pressure,
& give me free medicine, whenever
you come to visit. And what would be ideal
is if you marry a dentist, who can check my teeth.

DESTROYED BY A HABIT

If you'll only learn not to pick your nose
in public places, Mother said, I'm sure you'll be
a success in this world. Your girlfriends
aren't going to like it. They'll think
if he does it in public, imagine how many times
he must do it in private. Your boss won't want
to shake your hand, no matter how good a job
you do. Everyone will shun you. If you do it
when no one is looking, then no one will care.
But if you do it in front of people, they'll think
he must be making some kind of a statement—like
he never had a mother—which is certainly not true.

CAN'T IMAGINE WHAT SHE'LL SEE

When I get old, Mother said, I'd
rather live in a nursing home
than move in with you & your wife,
because I don't want to spend my time
wondering what she sees in you, &
she must have seen something, or
she wouldn't have married you.
And I hope for your sake that she
keeps seeing what she was seeing,
because once she stops, she might try to see it
in another man. So you should try to find out
what she likes about you, & then enlarge
that side of your personality, or
if it's something physical, like your
physique, then be sure not to gain any weight.
They say love is blind, but in your case
it also has to be deaf if she
is to put up with all your complaining.

THE PATH

The shortest distance between
her shoulders & her waist
was through her breasts,
so I paused there on my way
to finding out whether I was
going to spend the night
over her place or get sent home.

WE COULDN'T WORK IT OUT

Before she finished telling what a jerk
I was, I got tired of chewing my gum,
so I took it out of my mouth, wrapped it
in a piece of paper, & stuck it in my pocket,
& she said, "You see, you're more interested
in what you're doing than in what I have to say,"
& I said, "The flavor went out of it," &
she said, "You could have waited until I was
        finished speaking."

MAKING A GOOD IMPRESSION

I masturbated two times
before we went out on the date,
so I wouldn't look horny.

BEFORE YOU WERE BORN

I hope you're not one of those sons,
Mother said, who as soon as he leaves
the house, forgets that he has a mother.
And if I give you a kick every now & then
to keep you in line, just remember that
when I was pregnant with you, it was you
who kicked me first. I'd eat two ice creams
for dessert, one for me, the other for you,
but instead of swallowing it, like a normal fetus
should do, you just kept your mouth shut.
And when I went to see the pediatrician, &
he told me that I was gaining too much weight,
& had to watch my diet, I tried to eat
nothing, but then you'd start to kick.
And I couldn't wait for you to be born,
so I could smack you & get you back.

LATE TALKER

When you were three you didn't talk,
Mother said. So we took you to a doctor,
who told us not to worry, that you'll talk
when you're ready. The next year you
started to talk. Now we can't shut you up.
We keep remembering the good old days,
& wonder why we wanted you to change.
You were better behaved. You couldn't talk back.

A YEAR YOUNGER

If you don't do your chores,
Mother said, I won't let you
have a birthday party, & instead
of being nine, you'll be eight
for another year, & none of your
friends will want to play with someone
younger than them, & the school will leave you back,
& you'll have to repeat the same boring classes,
& while everyone is getting older, you'll
be staying the same, & you'll never
be able to catch up with them,
since you can't have two birthdays
in one year, because we couldn't
afford to buy you two presents.

MEMORIES

These are the best years of your life,
Mother said, so I suggest you slow down
while you're eating your chocolate cake.
And you should do worthwhile things,
like helping me clean the house,
so when you get older, you'll have memories
you can talk about. Because when
you get a girlfriend, & she tells you
about the times she helped her mother
do the dishes, & vacuum the rug,
you won't have anything to tell her, &
she'll think, He must lead a boring life,
& if I marry him he probably won't remember
the years he spent with me either.

DREAMS OF COATS

Whatever you do during the day
gets into your dreams, Mother said,
so that's why I'm not talking
to your father, because I'm tired
of waiting on him, & being treated
worse than a servant, & I want
to dream of pleasant things, like
wearing a fur coat, & not of having
a conversation with a cheapskate,
& if he starts talking to you, it's because
I'm not talking to him, so don't
say anything to him, & maybe he'll
get so lonely he'll buy me
a mink coat, so he can get to talk to me again.

READING MATTER

My parents got me a dictionary
for a birthday present. Mother said
if I learned five new words
every day, at the end of the year
I'll know more than a thousand new words,
& I'll be able to speak English
as if it's a foreign language,
& have no trouble being understood
if I ever go to Europe.
I tried reading it from beginning to end,
but got bored in the "A" section.
I used some new words
at the dinner table: *aardvark,*
admirable. But she said I was
just showing off, & very cultured people
sneak big words into their conversation
without anyone realizing that they did it.

CLOSE QUARTERS

I don't know why, Father said,
your mother picked this cemetery
for us to be buried in.
I'm not even under the ground,
& already I don't like it.
All the trees look so dismal
with their twisted branches.
They can't be from around here,
they must be imported. And look
at the row of tombstones.
They're so tightly packed against
each other that you can't walk
among them without feeling cramped.

DRESSED IN BLACK

These cowboy movies are all the same,
Father said. The good guy wears white,
& always wins. The bad guy dresses
in black, & always loses. Just once
I'd like to see the bad guy take
the woman & ride off with her
into the distance. Their marriage
might even last. Since all he wears
are dark colors she'll have
an easier time washing his clothes.

WHITE ON BLACK

The snow stayed in her hair
longer than my "I love you"
stayed on her mind.

NO REASON TO STAY

I've been out of college for only a year,
she said, & already there's practically nothing
that I haven't tried. I had a gay love affair,
fell in love with an older man (he was also
an alcoholic), got beaten up by my father,
& took a lot of drugs. My only failure
was my one suicide attempt. And if my boyfriend
wasn't around to stop me, I'd have been successful.
The only thing left for me to do was to have
a relationship with someone like you.
(You're not odd, just a little bit unusual.)
And now that I've accomplished that, though it wasn't
always easy, I guess it's time for me to leave.

THIEVES AMONG US

Don't count the money in your wallet,
Mother said, while someone is looking.
It might give him ideas. He'll want to steal it.
People are bad enough by themselves. They
don't need you to encourage them to act even worse.
You should know how much you have before you leave
the house. And you shouldn't carry a lot of change
in your pocket, because it'll make noise,
& someone will think that you are rich, & he'll
want to rob you. And if he steals from you,
then he's stealing from me, since I'll have to replace it.

DIFFERENT VERSIONS

The difference between the Christians
& the Jews, Mother said, is that they have
Jesus, who spoke in parables, & we have
Moses, who spoke in commandments. None
of them spoke in English, because
they lived in the desert, & Lawrence of Arabia,
who gave English lessons when he wasn't
fighting, wasn't born yet. We started
our religion first, & then they copied us. They
claimed that they improved on the Bible by adding
the New Testament. But you & I know that when
you try to improve on something by making it
bigger, like putting more bread crumbs in the
     meat loaf,
it's never as good as if you just left it alone.

CONCENTRATION

You have to concentrate when you go
to the bathroom, Mother said, or you'll
be sitting there for a half hour
with nothing to show for it. And you'll
develop hemorrhoids before you're an
old man, & everyone will know that
you have them, because of the way
that you sit. I know you have to go,
because I smelled something while we
were watching TV, & it had to be you,
because it definitely didn't come from me,
& your father denied having anything
to do with it, & he sometimes lies,
but never about something like that.

MISSING BODY

Don't go swimming in the ocean, Mother said,
right after you eat lunch. You could get
a cramp, & drown. You can't expect
the lifeguard to save you. He may not
have noticed that you went into the water,
he might have been too busy trying to remove
the sand from his hair. We may never find
your body, it could drift further out
into the sea, & not come back with the tide.
But I'll still get a tombstone for you,
& make it look like you're in the grave.
I just won't tell anyone that you're not there.

BEHIND THE DOOR

Don't open the door if you hear someone
knocking, Mother said, unless you know who it is.
It could be a robber. He'll thank you
for letting him in, & then he'll rob you.
He'll steal all our valuables, & whatever
is not nailed down. He could steal the nails too,
if he brought a hammer with him. He might
kidnap you. You're not worth very much,
but he may not know that, & could want thousands
of dollars for you. And we'll have to pay him, because
I need you back, so I can yell at you for opening
    the door.

PROSPECTIVE BRIDE

I don't know why you don't want us to meet
your girlfriend, Mother said. Of course,
if she doesn't exist, & you're making her up,
then I can understand your reasoning.
But if she's flesh & blood, don't you think
it would be nice for her to meet people?
I don't know what you do with each other
the whole day in that small apartment of yours.
I'm afraid to ask, but doesn't it get boring?
I'll make her a special dinner. She doesn't have
to like my cooking. All she has to do is eat it.
We promise not to say anything that'll make you
look bad. We want to lose you. We don't want you
hanging around to remind us we're getting older.

NEVER THOUGHT IT WOULD HAPPEN

When we were in bed you kept changing
your grip on my penis, first holding it
like a hammer, & then letting it rest
in your hand, until you lost interest
in it, because you kept waiting for me
to do something, but I was still shocked
that you were there in the first place.

ALWAYS GIVING COMMANDS

She bit my ear, & said, "Fuck me."
But that's what I thought I was doing.

 99

EVEN THE BIRDS ARE QUIET
SOMETIMES

Let's play hide & seek, Mother said.
You can hide anywhere in the house
while I do the laundry, & if
I don't find you, I'll have peace,
& if I discover your hiding place,
we'll start all over again. You think
the more noise you make, the more fun
you're having, but you can also have fun
with your mouth closed. I don't want
to have to wait until I'm dead
for peace & quiet, because then it'll be too late
for me to appreciate it, so let me have a little now.

HEAVEN BOUND

When I'm dead, Mother said, I'd appreciate it
if you prayed for me. Do it in Hebrew
& English, so God will hear it twice.
Let's hope that I won't need it, that I'll
get to heaven right away. But it could
take me days to get there, not every place
is close to New York. It'll be hard for me
to pray for myself, because I'll be without my body,
& will be a little disoriented. Though, it'll be
a big relief to be finally free of all that weight.

ADVICE ON FALLING

Don't walk over a subway grating,
Mother said. It might be loose,
& you could fall through & break a leg.
And if you happen to be quick enough
to stick your hand out in time
to soften your blow, then you'll break
your arm instead, but try to use your left one,
since you're right-handed. The first day
it'll be fun to wear a cast.
Everyone, including me, will want to sign it,
but then you're going to run out of space,
& your friends who were absent from school that day
will be mad at you for not saving them a spot.

POKED-OUT EYE

Don't stick your head out the window,
Mother said, while your father is driving.
A branch from a tree can poke out
your eye, & even if he stops in time,
& is able to find it among all the fallen leaves,
you can't just put it back into the socket,
& expect it to work like it did before.
A doctor will have to reconnect the tissues,
& if any part is damaged—your father
might have stepped on it before finding it—
it'll never work right, & everyone
will know that it's defective,
because of the way that you squint.

GET A JOB

Your eyes are red, Mother said.
You've probably been taking drugs again.
The next time that you do, you should
give me some. I could use sleeping pills.
I've been having trouble sleeping, worrying
about you. You're the only one in your class
not working this summer. When I meet
the mothers of your friends, they ask me
what you do, & when I say
you've been reading, they wonder why
you can't do it at night after working
during the day. You're not satisfied
just being a bum, but have to sit
in your room all day studying how to be a better one.

BANG BANG I SHOT HER DEAD

Just because your father didn't know
what he got you for your birthday present,
Mother said, doesn't mean that he didn't
buy it. He bought it at the store without
being there, by giving me the money.
He's an equal partner. The present is
half his. It's true that he didn't have
to navigate his way through the aisles, grab
the last cowboy gun off the shelf
while a woman twice his size was eyeing it,
& then stand in line. He didn't have to do
any of those things. So why have you
been testing your new gun out on me, & not him?

WASHCLOTH

Father came home from work
to find his son had stopped using a washcloth.
His wife felt there were too many parts of the back
the hand could never reach.
He took her side,
because he found it more peaceful to agree with her.
He didn't know why his son couldn't do what he did,
wet the washcloth but never use it.

WASTING TIME

If I knew you weren't interested in me
I wouldn't have wasted all those nights
masturbating about you. I'd have fantasized
about someone a lot more inaccessible,
like Madonna, so when a week later I found myself
still alone in bed, I wouldn't have been disappointed.

SUBMERGING

Sex, for me, became like swimming.
I didn't want to go into the water.
I wanted to stand outside & watch.
But once you pushed me in, I wouldn't
leave until you pulled me out.

AT THE ZOO

Your father & I didn't have to go to the zoo,
Mother said. We've seen enough animals
in our lifetime. But we did it for you.
We hope that when you're older you'll remember
the sacrifices we made. So I can't understand
how you can still be mad at us for not
letting you have an ice cream cone. The purpose
of the trip was not to have fun. We could
have done that in front of the television set.
We took you there so that when we're dead
you can't say we never took you anywhere.

HAPPY OR SAD

When you're happy, Mother said, I'm
happy. And when you're sad, I'm sad,
so if you have a choice between being
happy or sad, you should stop always
thinking about yourself, & think about me
for a change, & be happy. And if
you have no choice, & have to be
sad, then don't spend the whole day
moping, but get it over with, so
you & I can be happy again.

PUNISHING YOURSELF

All work & no play, Mother said,
makes you into a dull boy. And
then the mothers of your friends
will think I'm dull too, & won't want
to talk to me. You should go out
of the house once in a while to see if
the world is still there. If you
sit around all day you'll become
a bitter person, like the old woman
who lived in a shoe. She could have
moved into a larger place, like a boot,
but she stayed where she was, probably
because she was mad at her mother,
& wanted to punish her, but you don't
hurt anybody but yourself if you
make your own life miserable.

BROKEN WINDOW

They say broken glass means good luck,
Mother said, so when you broke the window
playing baseball I tried not to get upset,
& thought you might be trying to do me
some good, but after spending an hour
on my hands & knees picking up the pieces,
& not being able to walk around in my socks,
because I might have missed some,
I decided that I want nothing from you,
so don't try to bring me any more luck,
just play ball in front of your friend's house.

LOOSE BELT

You were born into this world naked,
Mother said, but that doesn't mean you
have to walk around with your pants
falling down. You should wear your
belt a notch tighter. You're not going
to make a good impression on a woman
if she's able to see some of your tushie
before she knows your name. She'll think,
If he's showing me his rear end, then he probably
wants me to show him mine, & she won't
want to have anything to do with you.

A SNOWBALL IN AUGUST

Don't put any snow in the icebox,
Mother said. You'll just have to wait,
like everyone else, for the next snowstorm,
to get more. And even though it will
give you a thrill to hit your friend
with a snowball when it's ninety degrees
outside, his mother won't be too happy
when she feels the bump on his head,
because the snow will have turned to ice.
She'll yell at me, & accuse me
of raising a future criminal. And I can't
claim that I'm innocent, because
as a mother I'm responsible for everything
that enters & leaves my refrigerator.

MOVING TRAIN

You should never walk around while the train
is moving, Mother said. You could fall,
& crack your kneecaps. You'll have to stay
in a hospital, & have surgery. And your father
may decide not to put a TV in your room,
so you'll have nothing to look at. Because
if we make it too pleasant for you,
you might decide to break something else.

HARMFUL SUN

When you go to the beach, Mother said,
I want you to stay out of the sun.
I read that if you get frequent sunburns
you'll end up with skin cancer. It
may hurt at first to watch your friends
frolicking in the water while you're
underneath a beach umbrella, but
just keep reminding yourself that when
you're all seventy they'll be dying
from skin cancer, & you'll probably
be dying from something else, but at least
it'll be internal, & no one will know what it is.

TUMBLING DOWN

Jack & Jill went up the hill, Mother said,
to fetch a pail of water, but they
both came tumbling down, because they listened
to their mother only on the way up, & not
on the way down. So I hope you
remember everything that I've told you
even after I'm dead, because the times
may change, but people always stay the same.
I don't care how advanced women become,
if you don't comb your hair, they'll stop
going out with you, because they'll get to thinking,
He must be testing me, & if I let him
get away without parting his hair,
the next time I see him he won't take a bath.

NOT TONIGHT

She said that I couldn't go back
with her to her place, because
she had to study for a test. And
that I wouldn't be able to help her,
because I wasn't good at mathematics.
The only thing I was good at was
taking off her clothes, but
she already knew how to do that.

OUTSIDE THE GATE AT THE CHILDREN'S ZOO

Looking at the overdressed scarecrow
at the Children's Zoo—it can't scare
anything away, including my thoughts
about you. I can hear the music
of the merry-go-round in the background,
& I remember how you loved to smile
at children. You were trying to convince me
how good you would be with them
if we had any. We never did.
Your diaphragm stayed in place,
& sometimes my sperm would trickle down your leg.

INVENTING JOBS

You're almost thirty, Father said,
& you don't have a job. When people
ask me what you're doing I make up
a job for you. And I have to remember
what I tell them, & not give you
a new job every week, or they'll get
suspicious. And if you do find a job,
& people tell me that I said you were working
at one store but they saw you at another, I'll be
so happy that you're finally standing on your own
two feet that I won't mind if they think I'm a liar.

SEPARATED SEATS

Your mother & I went to the movie theater,
Father said. It was very crowded,
& they told us that only single seats were left.
We agreed not to sit together. I forgot
to give her a ticket. I found a seat
between two women. The usher wouldn't
let your mother in. Thirty minutes
into the movie I see your mother
walking down the aisle between two ushers
with flashlights. She saw me sitting between
two women, eating popcorn, & laughing—
it was a comedy, I wasn't supposed to cry.
I didn't hear the end of it for two weeks.

ADVICE ON MONEY

Some women are going to be after your money,
Father said. And just because you don't
have any is not going to stop them.
They'll wait until you get some,
then they'll take it. So it's good practice
never to tell a woman how much you make.
Or in your case never tell her how much
you're going to make. You should marry someone
like your mother. She didn't care how much
I made. She loved me for myself. But she'd
count how much I had. She wanted to be
sure I wasn't giving it to another woman.

BIBLE HISTORY

Christ was Jewish, Father said, & then
he became Catholic. I never read
the New Testament, because I haven't
finished the old one yet, but I know
that he got mad at the Jews, & overturned
some tables at a temple. Now if I didn't
like the way my rabbi did things, I'd
just join another congregation, but it was
different in those days, there was only one
temple per town, & they didn't have
a reform, conservative, & orthodox branch,
like they do today, so he had to create a new religion.

OTHERS HAVE IT WORSE

You should thank your lucky stars,
Father said, that you weren't born a cripple.
So no matter how bad you think your life is,
cheer up, because some people have it worse. Imagine
having to hop to the bathroom, & urinate on one leg.
If you're not careful, you could fall
into the bowl. Then you'll have to yell
for someone to help you out. So you should
be grateful for what you have, & not complain
if things don't work out the way you wanted them to.
And if you get depressed, you can always
walk into the next room, & turn on the TV.
But if you were a cripple, getting to the next room
would be a major production. You'll be
dependent on someone to get you there, & to take
    you back.

CHANGING DOLLARS TO PENNIES

I brought my knife to school, Father said,
& carved a picture on my desk. The principal
told me that I couldn't graduate unless I
gave him five dollars to fix it. My
parents gave me the money, which was
a lot in those days. I went to the bank,
& changed it to 500 pennies. I placed them
inside a paper bag, & knocked on the principal's door.
I poured the pennies on his desk,
& told him that I raided my piggy bank.
I thought he'd feel sorry for me, & tell me
to keep my money. But he told me that he couldn't
accept the pennies, that I had to go to a bank,
& bring him five dollars. He was a tough guy.

HOW TO WASH CLOTHES

Just before your mother died, Father said,
she took me into the laundry room,
& showed me how to do a wash. She
had me put the five quarters in,
then showed me the button to push.
She wouldn't let me go upstairs,
but made me wait until the machine
was finished. It was like being stuck
in a car behind an eternal red light.
Then she showed me how to operate
the dryer. She wanted me to become
more independent. It worked. I don't
have to get married again.

EXPERIMENTING WITH HERBS

I drove my girlfriend to her boyfriend's grave,
Father said. She asked me to get out of the car,
& come with her, but I stayed inside. I figured
that what she had to say to him was personal,
& I didn't want to get in the way. Whatever
I say to her makes her smile. She helps me
with my prostate. She recommends a lot
of different herbs, like saw palmetto. I like her
a lot. She likes me enough to talk about her bladder.

TIMING

After we made love we went out
for dinner. I tried not to eat
my linguine faster than her. I
figured that if we couldn't have
a simultaneous orgasm we could
at least finish eating at the same time.

ABOUT THE AUTHOR

Hal Sirowitz lives in Flushing, New York. He was awarded a National Endowment for the Arts Fellowship. He has appeared on MTV's *Spoken Word Unplugged*, PBS's *The United States of Poetry*, NPR's *All Things Considered*, and the Lollapalooza Festival. He's on several compilation albums, *Poem Fone* (Tomato Records), *Relationships from Hell* (Big Deal Records), and *Grand Slam: The Best from the National Slam* (Nuyo Records).